THAT FLUFFY BITCH
STORIES & POEMS FOR YOUR FAVORITE DICKHEAD DOG

It's a beautiful fucking day to read a book
— LINDA

LINDA KING

www.thatfluffybitch.com

Copyright © 2019 Linda King

All rights reserved.

ISBN: 9781070462066

OH HAIR, OH HAIR
'THE FUCK.
ITS EVERYWHERE.

This precious little book is dedicated to our fluffy-bummed best friend, Audie.
The best dog we could ever ask for who somehow both loves and hates
every human on the planet simultaneously.
Our love for her is bigger than the galaxy,
and her attitude is bigger than us all.
Send help.

TABLE OF CONTENTS

Chapter One   It's not that big of a book, I think you'll survive navigation without assistance.

                                     You lazy fucks.

ACKNOWLEDGMENTS

A stellar thank you to Raf King - chief editor and co-parent of Audie (That fluffy bitch). And, of course, thank you to Audie for being the inspiration and the reason we spend a zillion dollars a month on toys and food that go under appreciated. Much love.

Enjoy.

PRINCESS JERKFACE

There once was a little princess
with hair as gold as hay

who dreamt of but one thing
day after fucking day.

Food, it's my fucking food.
That's what she wants.

BLESSED BE

Blessed be the parent of a dog.
To love a thing so sweet.

Until the pain o' thousand dagger claws
are unleashed upon your feet.

You fuzzy fuck.

GOODNIGHT MY ANGEL

Sweet slumber waits
on clouds of feathered bliss.

Sheets of satin weave
and a goodnight bedtime kiss.

And rest comes quick
to the heads that heavy be

'till that bitch wakes us up again
for the millionth time to pee.

'A' IS FOR ASSHOLE

A is for asshole.
Specifically, yours.

The
one
you
keep
scraping
across
all
my
floors.

'B' IS FOR BULLSHIT

B is for bullshit.
As in, 'I'm tired of your bullshit.'

MURDER AT MIDNIGHT

Dead.

On the carpet floor.
The blood, the gore.

Unbearable.

The agony we'd feel
if that poor stuffed bunny was real.

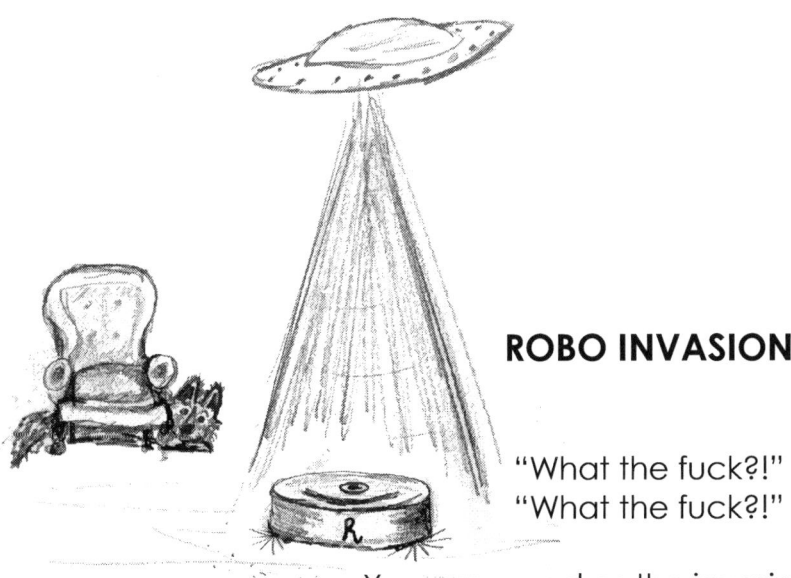

ROBO INVASION

"What the fuck?!"
"What the fuck?!"

You screamed as the invasion began.

It's only an exploratory drone this time,

gathering samples of debris
no doubt to take back to the mothership for analysis.
Followed by an overtaking of our home.

We must prepare for war.

THAT TIME YOU ATE MY CHILI

Oh shit.

NO REGRETS

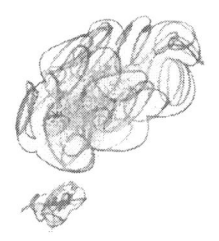

One sheep, two sheep,
dead sheep, blue sheep.

A monster lurks below.

Feasting on the plastic eyes of lambs,

proud of its destruction.

Fluffy white innards strewn across the lands.

RUNAWAY

Hey, remember that time you ran away?
That was super fucking rude.
And how I had to chase you?

For like a mile.

With no shoes.

Dick.

THE BATTLE OF DISHWASHER COVE

The roar o' hundred waves
a rumbling from the kitchen.

What bullshit noise is this
that causes my dog's bitchin'?

The sound of death, surely
from the look upon her face

as the deadly kitchen beast
cleans my cups and plates.

AMAZON WARRIOR

Like a smaller, fuzzier Godzilla,
you destroy.

Shredding.
Smashing.
Tearing apart.

You think it's fucking cute
to leave the carcass of my package
all over the floor.

DEATH BY DRYER

I'm sorry I offended you
by drying off my clothes.

I know it's late at night
and the laundry door won't close.

The noise must be unbearable
as I've gathered by your glare,

to wake you in the evening
is as rude as plucking hair.

SACRED GROUND

I see you wear the mud of your ancestors today.
A shit ton of it.

TOOT TOOT

Broccoli, beans, and cauliflower.
You stink so bad you need a shower.
Gods almighty wield their power.
Survive we won't, another hour.

BAD PARENTING

Once there was a fluffy pup
who really didn't give a fuck.

She warmed herself in daily sun
and murdered lizards just for fun.

She shit upon the neighbor's grass
and promptly told them, 'kiss my ass'

and when the day was settling down
she'd yell, 'fuck off' to all the town.

THAT SOUND YOUR MOUTH MAKES

I am aware of the sound
that comes from a grooming hound
as they lick themselves clean.
I hate it the most
because its fucking gross
and it makes me want to scream.

OH, FAIR MAIDEN

Once upon a time...

There was a golden princess who lived in her very own castle.

But this was no ordinary princess.

No,

this bitch had to eat organic,

grain free meat tubes with fancy blueberries and shit.

Because she's special.

YOU CREEP

I've never told you this

but there's truly something grand

about the way you trim

the tiny swords upon your hand.

Still it's kind of creepy

when you use your teeth to gnaw

the swords upon your hand

with the swords up in your jaw.

NEIGHBORS

"Fuck you!"
"I'll fuck you up!"

Whoa bitch, calm down.
They aren't even outside right now.

ENEMY OF MY ENEMY

It comes as no surprise
that you've thrown a fit again

after sitting in the corner
for chewing on my pen.

I'm not so shocked to see
The ink upon the wall

or the ink upon my vanity
and up and down the hall.

You think I am the enemy
but it's plain enough to see,

the one you mustn't trust
is the cat that told on thee.

YOU'RE BETTER THAN THIS

You're so fucking cute,
I love you.

You're so fucking smart,
it's true.

You're so fucking cool,
I know this.

So why the fuck
do you eat your poo?

FREAK

The clock strikes time.
You jump and rear,
mom and dad are nearly here.

You jut and zoom and
burn the rubber
and prove to be a zealous pupper.

If we'd have known
would we have owned
such a crazy motherfucker?

IT'S THE LITTLE THINGS

I love the way you
spin and twirl

just like you were a
little girl.

Frolic, bounce, and
have a hoot,

until you fart
it's all real cute.

PARENTAL WISDOM

When you yell at me, I feel compelled
to fuck you up.

Bitch, check yourself.

As mothers often say
to their younglings.

YOUR WEIGHT IN GOLD

A visit to the vet,
they tell us don't forget:

your weight's a bit to high
so you're likely more to die.

But what they cannot see
is that your beautiful to me
and you won't stop fucking begging.

TWO PEAS IN A POD

You and I are alike
in many ways I'm told.

It's said by friends and family
that we are both so bold.

Our neighbors call us assholes,
our mailman runs away.

We sleep till after 1pm,
we'd gladly sleep all day.

But the grandest way we are alike
to my surprise, I laugh

is the fullness of our golden hair
and our unladylike mustache.

EAT YOUR GRASS, BITCH

I saw you eating grass
to help your dinner pass.

So I grew this just for you
to help you when you poo.

You ate it for a moment
but your time was better spent

eating weeds right next to
the grass I grew for you.

Dick.

CHEERS TO YOU

A child is born
so beautifully.

So fragile a thing to hold.

And then there's you
upon the rug.

So farty, cute, and old.

IN TRUTH

If we're being honest
I think you need to know

the hardest truth of all
is that someday you'll go.

You're the fucking best
and truly I believe

that better than a human
my dog will always be.

THE END.

ABOUT THE AUTHOR

Linda King is an author and artist in northern Arizona with a passion for evoking emotions from her readers and viewers. Her mission is to imagine, create, and inspire with such passion that it sparks another's flame and to imagine a future so bold that when she finally creates it, she'll inspire the world.

She spends her days in bliss with her husband and dog.

Made in the USA
Lexington, KY
28 September 2019